God Given Friends

God Given Friends

JOHN ALEXANDER

DEDICATION

Dedicated to those who cherish God given friends.

CONTENTS

ACKNOWLEDGEMENTS

I wish to acknowledge my wife for her patience and encouragement as I write and for her seeds of inspiration to get me started.

I want to thank the Mockingbird chapter of the Poetry Society of Texas for the feedback and encouragement to continue writing.

I want to acknowledge Craig and Karen Ruhl at Faith On Every Corner magazine who allow me to share my poems around the globe as part of their monthly magazine.

A special offer of thanks and gratitude goes out to friends in the Marathon Class and the Men's Bible study group for their interest and encouragement as I continue to write.

A thank you goes out to friends and followers on QuietTimeRhymes.com and Facebook who are a constant stream of encouragement as they read my words, offer comments, and share their support.

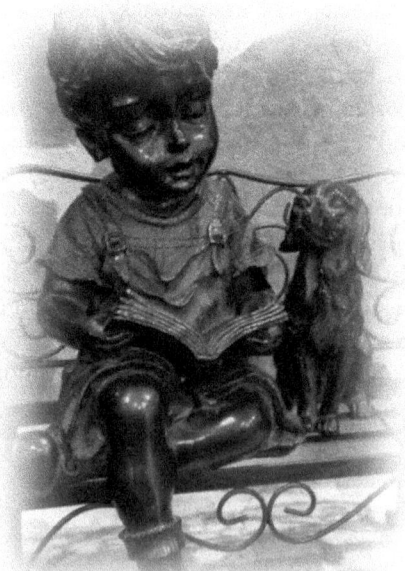

GENTLE - STRONG

Lord help direct my words today.
It's not just things I long to do,
But also, what I choose to say,
That should align and both be true.

When I mess up, I make amends,
But can't erase the things I've said.
But words like kind and gentle friends
Can give encouragement and spread.

I pray for wisdom and control
Of words I use and what I say.
"Lift others up" should be my goal.
I pray that's true of me today.

Lord help me be both gentle, strong,
Share words that linger like a song.

FRIENDS

I cherish all my friends who pray,
Who hear my words, care what I say.
They share a laugh or shed a tear.
When I'm in need a friend is near.

Surrounded by so many prayers,
How can I feel the weight of cares?
We share a bond; we know the Lord.
We bow in prayer in one accord.

We fellowship; we share our heart.
We give support when we're apart.
They're at my side to lift me up,
To keep me going, fill my cup.

Though earthly friends may come and go,
There's one who's always true I know.
He's always there, my closest friend,
The Lord whose love will never end.

TIME WITH FRIENDS

Time alone to start my day,
To talk to God, to read and pray,
Help give each day a brand-new start,
But we're not made to live apart.

I value time I spend with friends.
It helps me see through different lens.
We each have traveled different roads.
We each have carried different loads.

We share our stories from the heart,
Remember them when we're apart.
The points of view we each reflect
Are different, yet we show respect.

We laugh and joke, we tell a few,
They're mostly old, but some are new.
It's something that I recommend,
Invest the time to make a friend.

A FRIEND

So many sources of despair,
Don't carry more than you can bear.
Surround yourself with words of hope,
Encouragement to help you cope.

I pray you know and trust a friend,
Someone on whom you can depend
To lend assistance to succeed.
Reach out for help when you're in need.

You too can be a trusted friend
To those in pain who need to mend,
If you're available to share,
Reach out in love to show you care.

Sometimes the hurt is deep inside,
Concealed and covered up with pride.
Sometimes it's hard, but wait and pray,
And God will lead, He'll show the way.

FRIENDSHIPS

I pray I'm never void of friends,
The ones who care through ups and downs,
The ones on whom I can depend.
Though miles apart they're still around,

The friends I've known for many years,
The ones brand new, those yet to find,
With whom I share both laughs and tears.
The years build up the bond that binds.

Some friendships form that never break,
Throughout the years endure and last,
Weather storms, life's give and take,
And share the future, present, past.

I'm grateful for the friends I've known,
I thank the Lord I'm not alone.

JOHN ALEXANDER

VALUE FRIENDS

I need my friends upon this earth.
They shelter me from scorching sun.
More valuable than gold is worth,
They sit with me when I can't run.

A friendship's roots grow thick and deep,
Tap wisdom deep beneath the ground.
Their loyalty does not come cheap.
In times of need a friend's around.

Those times when life gets hot and dry,
A friend provides much needed shade.
When life's unfair, I'm asking why,
It's then I cherish friends I've made.

Keep friendships fresh and make some new.
Spend time with friends and be one too.

NOT ALONE

If I lived on an island, was stranded alone,
Would I survive? Would my heart turn to stone?
Could I live without friends who provide love and care?
I'm not meant for an island with no one to share.

My friends share the good times, rejoice when I'm glad.
They're with me in sorrow whenever I'm sad.
My friends give encouragement, help me survive.
Refreshed by their friendship I'm fully alive.

Surrounded by friends I find comfort and hope.
The prayers of my friends lift me up, help me cope.
The Lord is our hope, and we all share His love.
Our hope is in glory, our home is above.

I pray that I too am considered a friend,
Return every kindness, help others to mend.

A CUP AND A FRIEND

It's nice to have some time to think,
Some solitude to sit and be.
But also, nice to share a drink,
Some coffee or a cup of tea,

With those we love, converse aloud,
Share stories of those yesteryears
When we were young and strong and proud,
Those memories that we hold dear.

Though through the years some friendships fade,
Lose track of those that we once knew,
As we share love, new friends are made.
We all could add at least a few.

I pray you'll always have a friend,
Someone on whom you can depend.

PRAYING FRIENDS

I thank the Lord for friends who pray
Not just for me but others too.
I also pray for you today.
I pray God richly blesses you.

Praise God for faithful caring friends.
We share good times and laugh a bit.
Upon your prayers I can depend.
I also love your smile, your wit.

Your heart is strong and also kind.
I'm grateful that our journey's shared.
Good friends like you are hard to find.
We lift each other up in prayer.

I'm grateful that we share God's love
And both will live with Him above.

LOVING FRIENDS

Can I still enjoy roses though pricked by a thorn?
Will laughter return once life's caused me to mourn?
Although in my life I've had good times and bad,
My peace soon returns, I don't have to stay sad.

No matter the wind and the storms life may bring,
The morning will dawn, and the birds will still sing.
Life's constantly changing each day is brand new.
I give thanks for each morning, I've seen quite a few.

I treasure the friends I have made through the years.
I can share with them laughter and also the tears.
Whenever I need them, I know they are there.
I'm eager to help them and lift them in prayer.

We're all getting older and showing our age.
Close friends are important at any life stage.
I pray you are covered by friends who will pray,
A blanket of love that will warm you today.

GOODBYE TO A FRIEND

It's hard to let go, say goodbye to a friend,
Sad that their days on this earth had to end.
So many fond mem'ries remain in our heart,
They'll linger forever and never depart.

Remember the good times enjoyed in the past,
Cherish those memories, hold to them fast.
I'm grateful for friends, we have all shared so much.
We lean on each other, no need for a crutch.

Together we honor the life of our friend,
Though no longer with us his life will not end.
In heaven he's frolicking, happy, carefree,
Beholding the beauty, there's so much to see.

We'll see him again just inside heaven's gate.
Together with Jesus, it's not long to wait.

JOHN ALEXANDER

A FRIEND'S COMFORT

Perhaps you're the one who needs comfort today,
Or perhaps it's another you help in some way.
We all need each other. We all need a friend.
Someone beside us to help us to mend.

Those times when we're hurting, feel helpless and lost,
Our friendships are priceless, not measured by cost.
We need someone beside us with whom we can share
Who'll soothe as they listen, give comfort and care.

Whether you or a friend is the one who's in need,
Either give or receive a kind word or a deed.
Those times when we're hurting, we also will learn
The value of comfort that we can return.

I know that no matter what you're going through
The Lord is a friend who'll bring comfort to you.

COMFORT

I thank you Lord that we can pray.
You know our needs, care what we say.
We lift up friends who mourn today,
On their behalf for them we pray.

You ease the pain of doubts and fears.
You offer comfort, dry the tears.
So many Lord must now adjust,
Renew their faith, renew their trust.

When those we love are now with you,
Lord grant us strength to start anew.
So many lives are different now,
Help them adapt, Lord show them how.

We pray their days won't seem so long.
Lord mend their hearts and keep them strong.
Lord help them find the joy you bring.
We pray that soon, once more they'll sing.

A FRIEND IN GRIEF

How do I help a friend in grief
When hope's been taken like a thief?
Does my response show love, respect,
Acknowledge pain and not reject?

Encouragement brought graciously,
Served up with sensitivity,
Can still at times not hit the mark,
If it's too soon, it's still too dark.

No cheerful words about the light
Are well received in dead of night.
It's not my place to question why,
Just share the pain and hear the cry.

Nor should I focus on a cure,
But rather help them to endure.
If I'm too busy being wise,
I'll fail to hear the mournful cries.

The grief will ease but needs some time.
At first the hill's too steep to climb.
Compassion listens, lets grief speak,
Provides the audience they seek.

Perhaps reach out and take their hand.
In silence show I understand.
Repeat the grief I hear them share,
As I lift words to God in prayer.

A SMILE

Sometimes it's the small things that lodge in my heart,
Perhaps just a smile, or a hug, or firm hand.
It's the warmth and the feelings such gestures impart,
Affirming assurance that friends understand.

It takes but an instant to show that we care.
A small act of kindness can go a long way,
And touch a heart deeper than we were aware.
Our words and our actions have much to convey.

If I'm true to myself, and I let others see,
If my heart is reflected by words that I choose,
I find when I share, I learn more about me.
I plan to keep sharing, I've nothing to lose.

I pray as I write that I'm sharing a smile.
Perhaps it will linger and stay for a while.

KINDNESS

We all can give others some kindness, respect,
A habit, when busy, we sometimes neglect.
It takes little effort, a nod or a smile.
When you give it a try you will find it worthwhile.

For someone in need, you can brighten their day.
It's amazing the kindness your words can convey.
It may be a stranger you pass on the street.
Perhaps it's a friend that you happen to meet.

Be careful the words that you use when you talk,
You don't know the pathway that others have walked.
Find ways to encourage with words from the heart.
Lift someone's spirit before you depart.

Some day when you're troubled, discouraged, or grieved,
I pray that same kindness is also received.

A PRAYER FOR YOU

I've reached an age considered old.
I've seen a lot of life unfold.
I'm grateful for the days and years,
For ups and downs, for joys and tears.

I've made some friends along the way,
I lift a prayer for you today,
And for the friends I'm yet to meet,
This prayer's for you to be complete,

"No matter what this day may bring,
That through it all your heart may sing.
"No matter what's your stage of life,
You've likely seen your share of strife.

"Those close to you with whom you share,
I pray will hear, show love and care."
I pray you find this prayer is true,
It wraps your heart, embraces you.

GROW JOY

I pray these simple words today
Will soothe your heart in some small way.
No matter what you're going through,
Or what you have in front of you,

I pray for strength to reach your goal.
I pray for peace inside your soul.
I pray new heights you can attain,
That your hard work is not in vain.

I pray you're loved by trusting friends,
On whom you always can depend.
I pray you share the life you live,
Each day you find a way to give,

To use the things you've done and know
To help another learn and grow.
As you find wisdom to impart,
I pray that joy grows in your heart.

I REMINISCE

Sometimes when life gets put on hold
From aches and pains of growing old,
I take some time to reminisce,
And think about the ones I miss.

Those special people I have known
Who shaped my life before I'd grown.
My parents, teachers, pastors, friends
Helped show me life seen through their lens.

So many folks no longer here,
Their memories I still hold dear.
When I grew up, I moved around.
I've traveled some, seen foreign towns.

The different places, people there
Have stretched my mind, I'm more aware
Conditions vary place to place,
But all still need God's love and grace.

COUNSEL FROM FRIENDS

Words can be passionate, strong and sincere,
Persuasively spoken and easy to hear,
But under the surface the motives are wrong.
It's more about power, exciting a throng.

Beware of an eloquent passionate speech
That tries to entice you, persuade you, beseech.
Examine the motives, the spirit, the heart.
Understand what you're doing before you take part.

Be wise as a serpent and take time to pray.
Examine the scriptures and see what they say.
Seek Godly counsel from friends who are wise.
Words spoken convincingly still can be lies.

I pray for wise leaders whose motives are pure,
Who love God and country to help us endure.

EACH PATH

We each one have a path to tread,
Sometimes we choose, sometimes we're led.
Some take us through some rough terrain.
The way at times we can't explain.

Sometimes it seems a lonely trail.
Who's there to catch me if I fail?
I value those who call me friend,
Who walk with me around the bend,

Who lend a hand when I'm in need,
Sometimes in word, sometimes in deed.
I'll have a chance along the way
To offer help some future day.

When no one's there to take my hand,
I know the Lord who always can.
He's always there close by my side,
And in His love, I can abide.

LISTENING

I'm not the most humorous, witty old chap.
I'm not full of great stories to make others laugh.
I'm not likely to speak just to fill in a gap,
Between listening and talking it's not half and half.

I love to hear stories that other folks tell,
Especially old folks who've lived a full life,
A look back at history they know it so well.
They remember the good times and also the strife.

We all have our stories, the good and the bad,
A stockpile of mem'ries we're building each day.
I pray there's some laughter to mix with the sad,
The sunshine that follows when rain comes our way.

Take time to listen, to make a new friend.
It's good for the soul. It will help a heart mend.

SHADOWS OF THE PAST

Turn around, turn around, have a look, and take heed.
Sift through the ashes, those days of the past.
Hold on to treasures that one day you'll need.
The substance is gone but the memories last.

The things that I do with my life every day,
The plans that I make and the hours that I spend,
The people I meet on the path 'long the way,
May turn into treasure, become a new friend.

The present and future are subject to change.
The days of the past provide context and form.
The shadows they cast may at times appear strange,
Whether blue skies and sunshine or those that bring storms.

Each day in our album we add a new page.
We value our memories more as we age.

ALONE NOT FORGOTTEN

Find someone who's lonely, in need of a friend.
Ignored and forgotten it's easy to hide.
An invisible curtain begins to descend,
With no one to listen, just sadness inside.

If someone seems different and not like the rest,
It's easy to turn and pretend they're not there.
Someone hurting in silence won't likely protest,
Just continue assuming there's no one to care.

Perhaps it's some tragedy early in life,
That began a long journey of feeling alone.
If their shell is too thick to cut through with a knife,
Don't assume that inside is a heart made of stone.

Lord open my heart help me see through Your eyes,
Help me to hear those who silently cry.

SHARED MEMORIES

I'm always surprised I keep writing each day,
Mostly surprised I have something to say.
I'm not really shy, just not gifted with gab.
I'm more prone to listen, less likely to blab.

I guess I find writing more easily shared.
I can tinker with words forming lines that will pair.
I'm less likely to write what I'll later regret
With a chance to review, and revise 'til they're set.

With old friends there's no need for a backspace, erase.
There's nothing like friendship, a hug or embrace,
Swapping stories, remembering times from the past,
How even today we see shadows they cast.

Though not often together old friendships endure.
Hold onto the mem'ries and keep them secure.

JOHN ALEXANDER

PASSING THROUGH

I never know if this will be my final parting rhyme,
The day the Lord will call my name, provide a different home.
If today will mark the end of this my earthly time,
My spirit, soul set free again, throughout the heavens roam.

I value all the friends I've made throughout my earthly stay.
I know that I'm a stranger here, that I'm just passing through.
My home is with the Lord on high and I'll be called away.
That final phase provides for me a life forever new.

I thank the Lord each day I'm here for this my time on earth,
The beauty of creation that God put me here to see.
I'm grateful for each day I've spent, each day beyond my birth.
I'm grateful for each day of life the Lord has given me.

When my final chapter's done, there's no more left to tell,
I pray that I've accomplished all the things I should have done.
I pray that I have pleased the Lord and I have lived it well,
When He calls and says to me, "It's time, come home my son."

Lord lead the way and teach me Lord each day to follow you.
Help me Lord to seize each day, know things I've left to do.

PENNING WORDS

I pray I discern when my writing should end.
Are there any more words that my heart needs to share?
What more would I say sitting down with a friend,
Or in rhymes shared with others when I'm not aware?

I pray that the rhythm and rhyme of each line
Like a balm soothes the heart for a moment or two.
May the Lord bless the words, turning water to wine.
May His love in my soul be found also in you.

I can write from my heart as I pen words each day.
I can share what I find, what I read in His Word.
As I try to explain, use the right words to say,
I cannot control if the message is heard.

Lord help me keep writing, provide those who read,
As long as my words are still meeting a need.

SHARE WITH A FRIEND

My rhymes capture thoughts that I'd share with a friend.
I search for the words as I share from my heart.
Each has a beginning, a middle, and end.
The challenge is finding a good place to start.

If I try to embellish the words that I write,
Sometimes I get lost and I take the wrong trail.
If I keep my mind focused and never lose sight
Of the reason for sharing then words will prevail.

If my theme is uplifting and words that I pen
Help others find joy and God's peace in their soul,
Then I count it a victory, I call it a win.
If I've helped spread His light, I've accomplished my goal.

I pray you find comfort in words that I share.
Pass them on to another to show love and care.

ABOUT THE AUTHOR

I live in Frisco, Texas with my wife and our spoiled Caviler Spaniel, Lucy. I began writing rhymes in the spring of 2017. I began writing rhymes during my quiet time February 2020. Writing is my passion and I will continue to write more rhymes. I would love to hear from you. Visit my website, browse my blog, find me on Facebook and drop me a note.

Blessings,
John Alexander

QuietTimeRhymes.com
facebook.com/QuietTimeRhymes
john@QuietTimeRhymes.com

www.ingramcontent.com/pod-product-compliance
Lightning Source LLC
Chambersburg PA
CBHW060043040426
42331CB00032B/2261